THE BIBLE ATLAS

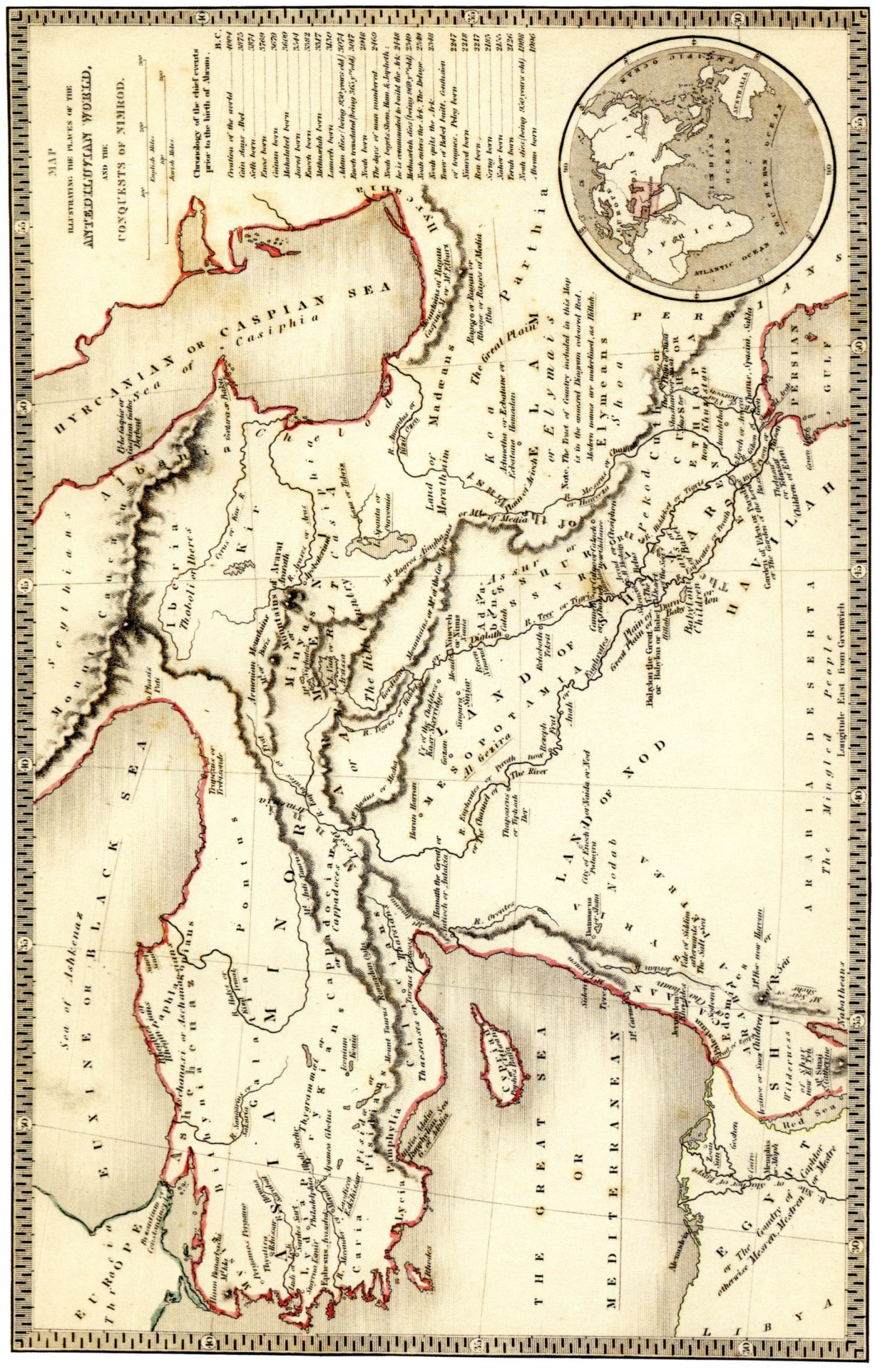

From *The Bible Atlas, with Ancient and Modern Names, being a Diliineation of the Geography, and a Chronological Arrangement of the History of the Holy Bible, as also of the Apocryphal Books and Josephus*, by Samuel Arrowsmith, Hydrographer to the King, London, 1835

THE BIBLE ATLAS

The Essential Guide to the Old and New Testaments

O. D. CASE

TMP

THIRD MILLENNIUM PRESS LIMITED

Published by
Third Millennium Press Ltd
Copyright © 2017 Third Millennium Press Ltd.,
Chippenham, England

Illustrations by permission of the Chamberlain Archive.
Inquiries to reproduce illustrated material should be
addressed to Third Millennium Press Ltd.,
Lowden Manor Cottage, Lowden Hill,
Chippenham, Wiltshire,
SN15 2BX, UK

ISBN: 978-1-86118-942-4

Printed in China.

CONTENTS

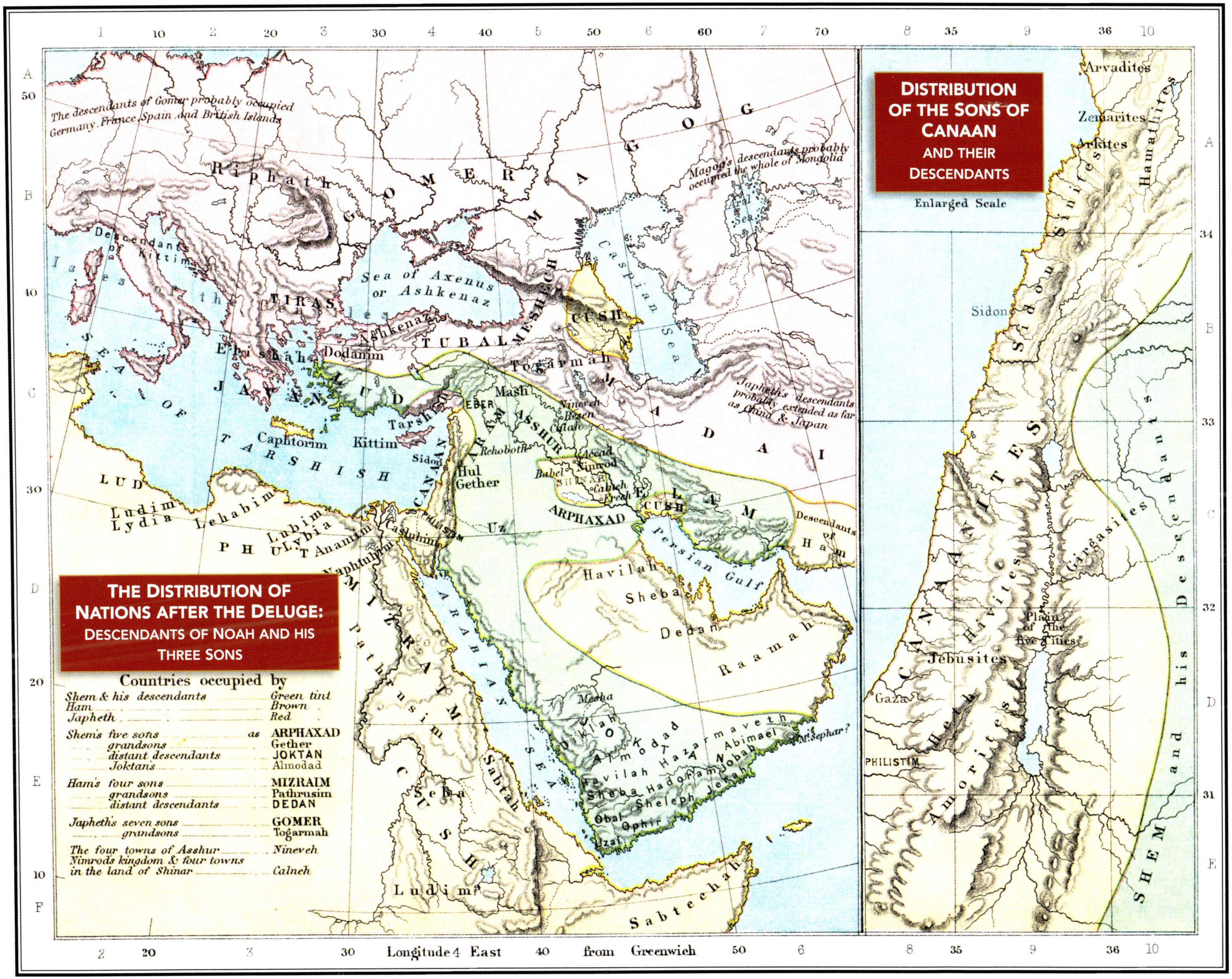

MAP 1

DISTRIBUTION OF THE SONS OF CANAAN AND THEIR DESCENDANTS

Enlarged Scale

Arvadites
Zemarites
Arkites
Hamathites
SHEM and his Descendants
Girgasites
Hivites
Sidon
Hittites
Perizzites?
Amorites
Jebusites
CANAAN
Gaza
PHILISTIM
Amorites

THE DISTRIBUTION OF NATIONS AFTER THE DELUGE: DESCENDANTS OF NOAH AND HIS THREE SONS

Countries occupied by

Shem & his descendants	Green tint
Ham	Brown
Japheth	Red

Shem's five sons as ARPHAXAD
grandsons — Gether
distant descendants — JOKTAN
Joktans — Almodad

Ham's four sons — MIZRAIM
grandsons — Pathrusim
distant descendants — DEDAN

Japheth's seven sons — GOMER
grandsons — Togarmah

The four towns of Asshur. — Nineveh
Nimrod's kingdom & four towns — Calneh
in the land of Shinar

The descendants of Gomer probably occupied
Germany, France, Spain and British Islands

Magog's descendants probably
occupied the whole of Mongolia

Japheth's descendants
probably extended as far
as China & Japan

Descendants of Ham

Caspian Sea
Sea of Axenus or Ashkenaz
GOG
MAGOG
RIPHATH
GOMER
MESHECH
TUBAL
Togarmah
Ashkenaz
Dodanim
ELISHAH
Kittim
JAVAN
Tarshish
ISLES OF TARSHISH
SEA OF KITTIM
Ludim
Lebabim
Lydia
Ludia
Anamim
PHILISTIM
Caphtorim
LUD
CANAAN
Sidon
Hul
Gether
LUD
ARAM
Uz
Mash
ASSHUR
EBER
Rehoboth
Babel
Erech
Accad
Calneh
ARPHAXAD
CUSH
Asshur
MIZRAIM
Pathrusim
MEDIA
ELAM
Havilah
Persian Gulf
Sheba
Dedan
Raamah
Sheba
Havilah
Joktan
Hazarmaveth
Almodad
Ophir
Obal
Sheleph
Jobab
Diklah
Sabtechah?
ARABIAN SEA
Sabtah
Seba
Sabtah
CUSH
Raamah
PUT

Longitude 4 East   from   Greenwich

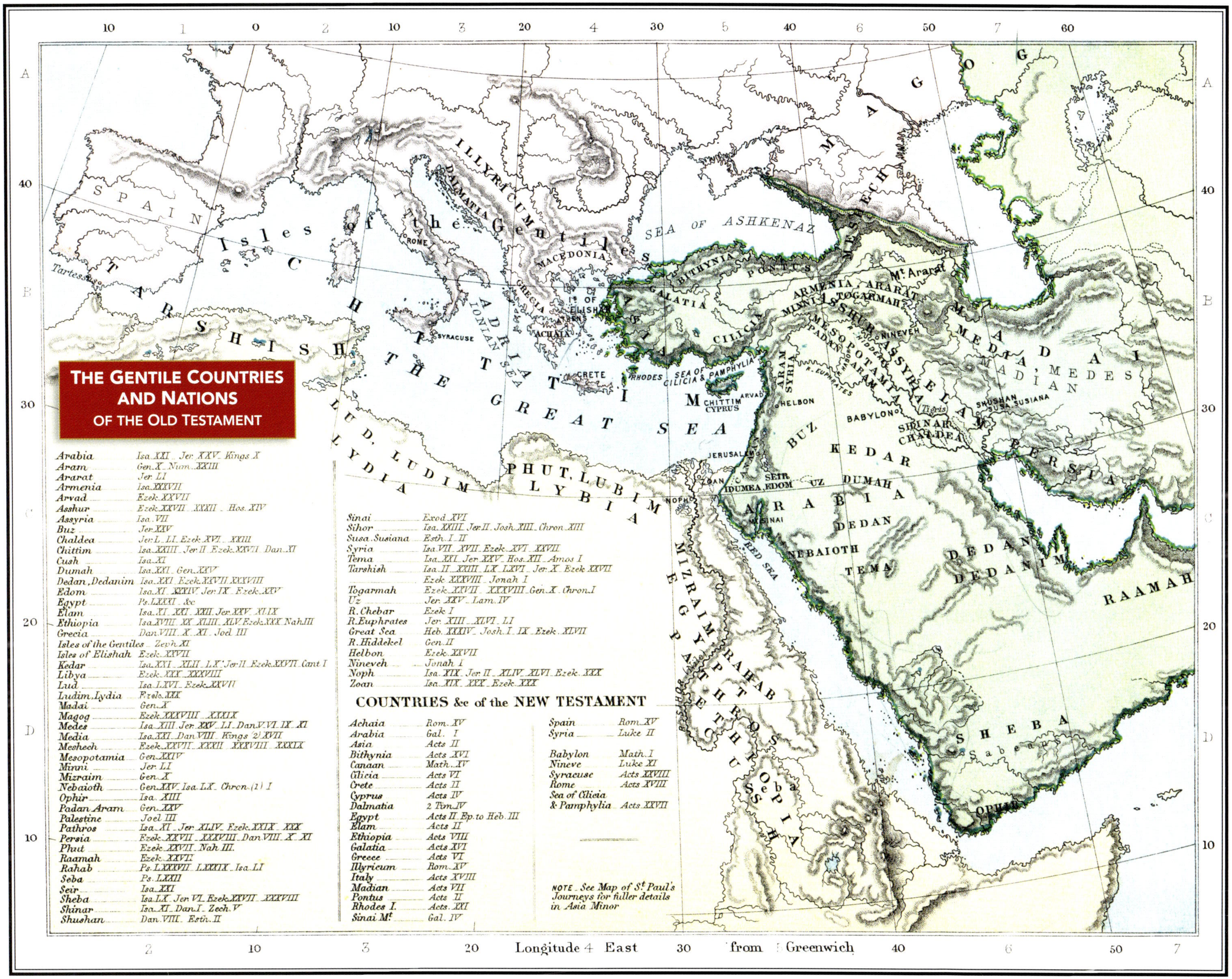
THE GENTILE COUNTRIES AND NATIONS
OF THE OLD TESTAMENT
Arabia Isa. XXI _ Jer. XXV _ Kings X
Aram Gen. X _ Num. XXIII
Ararat Jer. LI
Armenia Isa. XXXVII
Arvad Ezek. XXVII
Asshur Ezek. XXVII _ XXXII _ Hos. XIV
Assyria Isa. VII
Buz Jer. XXV
Chaldea Jer. L _ LI _ Ezek. XVI _ XXIII
Chittim Isa. XXIII _ Jer. II _ Ezek. XXVII _ Dan. XI
Cush Isa. XI
Dumah Isa. XXI _ Gen. XXV
Dedan, Dedanim Isa. XXI _ Ezek. XXVII XXXVIII
Edom Isa. XI _ XXXIV _ Jer. IX _ Ezek. XXV
Egypt Ps. LXXXI _ &c
Elam Isa. XI _ XXI _ XXII _ Jer. XXV _ XLIX
Ethiopia Isa. XVIII _ XX _ XLIII _ XLV Ezek. XXX Nah. III
Grecia Dan. VIII _ X _ XI _ Joel III
Isles of the Gentiles Zeph. XI
Isles of Elishah Ezek. XXVII
Kedar Isa. XXI _ XLII _ LX Jer. II _ Ezek. XXVII _ Cant I
Libya Ezek. XXX _ XXXVIII
Lud Isa. LXVI _ Ezek. XXVII
Ludim, Lydia Ezek. XXX
Madai Gen. X
Magog Ezek. XXXVIII _ XXXIX
Medes Isa. XIII _ Jer. XXV _ LI _ Dan. V _ VI _ IX _ XI
Media Isa. XXI _ Dan. VIII _ Kings (2) XVII
Meshech Ezek. XXVII _ XXXII _ XXXVIII _ XXXIX
Mesopotamia Gen. XXIV
Minni Jer. LI
Mizraim Gen. X
Nebaioth Gen. XXV _ Isa. LX _ Chron. (1) I
Ophir Isa. XIII
Padan Aram Gen. XXV
Palestine Joel III
Pathros Isa. XI _ Jer. XLIV _ Ezek. XXIX _ XXX
Persia Ezek. XXVII _ XXXVIII _ Dan. VIII _ X _ XI
Phut Ezek. XXVII _ Nah. III.
Raamah Ezek. XXVII
Rahab Ps. LXXXVII _ LXXXIX _ Isa. LI
Seba Ps. LXXII
Seir Isa. XXI
Sheba Isa. LX _ Jer. VI _ Ezek. XXVII _ XXXVIII
Shinar Isa. XI _ Dan. I _ Zech. V
Shushan Dan. VIII _ Esth. II
Sinai Exod. XVI
Sihor Isa. XXIII _ Jer. II _ Josh. XIII _ Chron. XIII
Susa, Susiana Esth. I _ II
Syria Isa. VII _ XVII _ Ezek. XVI _ XXVII
Tema Isa. XXI _ Jer. XXV _ Hos. XII _ Amos I
Tarshish Isa. II _ XXIII _ LX _ LXVI _ Jer. X _ Ezek. XXVII
Ezek. XXXVIII _ Jonah I
Togarmah Ezek. XXVII _ XXXVIII _ Gen. X _ Chron. I
Uz Jer. XXV _ Lam. IV
R. Chebar Ezek. I
R. Euphrates Jer. XIII _ XLVI _ LI
Great Sea Heb. XXXIV _ Josh. I _ IX _ Ezek. XLVII
R. Hiddekel Gen. II
Helbon Ezek. XXVII
Nineveh Jonah I
Noph Isa. XIX _ Jer. II _ XLIV _ XLVI _ Ezek. XXX
Zoan Isa. XIX _ XXX _ Ezek. XXX
COUNTRIES &c of the NEW TESTAMENT
Achaia Rom. XV
Arabia Gal. I
Asia Acts II
Bithynia Acts XVI
Canaan Math. XV
Cilicia Acts VI
Crete Acts II
Cyprus Acts IV
Dalmatia 2 Tim. IV
Egypt Acts II _ Ep. to Heb. III
Elam Acts II
Ethiopia Acts VIII
Galatia Acts XVI
Greece Acts VI
Illyricum Rom. XV
Italy Acts XVIII
Madian Acts VII
Pontus Acts II
Rhodes I. Acts. XXI
Sinai Mt. Gal. IV
Spain Rom. XV
Syria Luke II
Babylon Math. I
Nineve Luke XI
Syracuse Acts XXVIII
Rome Acts XVIII
Sea of Cilicia & Pamphylia Acts XXVII
NOTE _ See Map of St. Paul's Journeys for fuller details in Asia Minor
SPAIN
Tartessus
TARSHISH
Isles of the Gentiles
ILLYRICUM
DALMATIA
ROME
MACEDONIA
GRECIA
ACHAIA
ATHENS
SYRACUSE
ADRIA
IONIAN SEA
CRETE
RHODES
SEA OF CILICIA & PAMPHYLIA
CHITTIM
CYPRUS
ARVAD
THE GREAT SEA
LUD, LUDIM
LYDIA
PHUT, LUBIM
LYBIA
NOPH
ZOAN
JERUSALEM
SEIR
IDUMEA, EDOM
UZ
SINAI
RED SEA
MIZRAIM
EGYPT
PATHROS
RAHAB
ETHIOPIA
Seba
SEA OF ASHKENAZ
MAGOG
MESHECH
BITHYNIA
PONTUS
GALATIA
CILICIA
ARMENIA
ARARAT
Mt. Ararat
TOGARMAH
MINNI
ASSHUR
NINEVEH
MESOPOTAMIA
PADAN ARAM
ASSYRIA
R. EUPHRATES
ARAM
SYRIA
HELBON
BABYLON
SHINAR
CHALDEA
Tigris
ELAM
SHUSHAN
SUSA
SUSIANA
MADAI
MEDES
MEDIA
MADIAN
PERSIA
BUZ
KEDAR
DUMAH
ARABIA
DEDAN
NEBAIOTH
TEMA
DEDANIM
RAAMAH
SHEBA
Sabeans
OPHIR
Longitude East from Greenwich

MAP 2

THE EXODUS OR JOURNEYINGS OF THE ISRAELITES FROM EGYPT TO CANAAN

English Miles

MAP 3

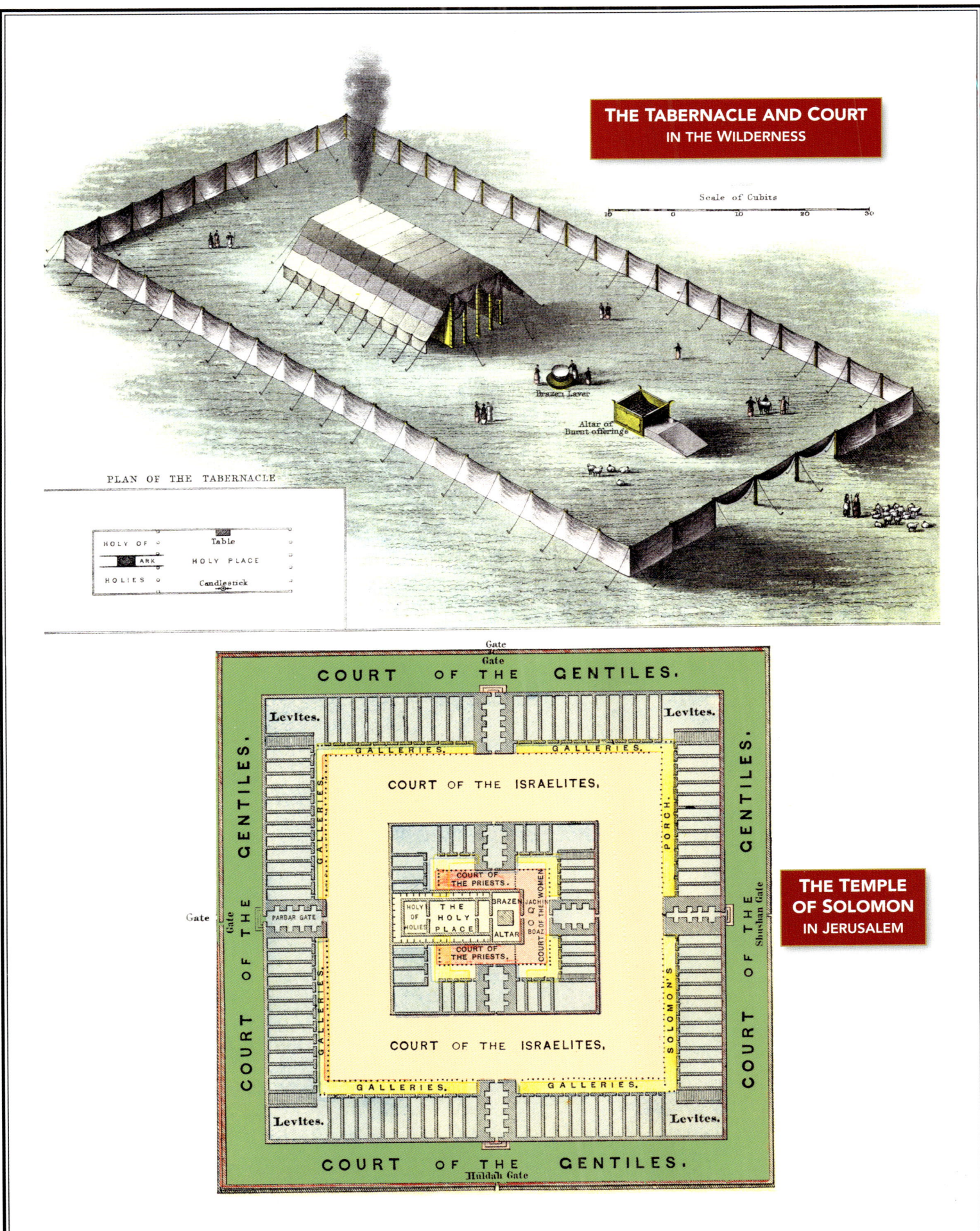

THE TABERNACLE AND COURT
IN THE WILDERNESS

Scale of Cubits

PLAN OF THE TABERNACLE

HOLY OF		Table
	ARK	HOLY PLACE
HOLIES		Candlestick

Brazen Laver

Altar of
Burnt offerings

Gate
Gate
COURT OF THE GENTILES.

Levites.
Levites.

GALLERIES.
GALLERIES.

COURT OF THE ISRAELITES.

COURT OF THE PRIESTS.
COURT OF THE WOMEN

HOLY OF HOLIES
THE HOLY PLACE
BRAZEN ALTAR
JACHIN
BOAZ

PARBAR GATE

COURT OF THE PRIESTS.

COURT OF THE GENTILES.
COURT OF THE GENTILES.
COURT OF THE GENTILES.
COURT OF THE GENTILES.

PORCH.
SOLOMON'S
Shushan Gate

Gate
Gate

THE TEMPLE OF SOLOMON
IN JERUSALEM

COURT OF THE ISRAELITES.

GALLERIES.
GALLERIES.

Levites.
Levites.

COURT OF THE GENTILES.
Huldah Gate

MAP 4

THE HOLY LAND
AS ALLOTTED BY JOSHUA TO THE
TWELVE TRIBES OF ISRAEL

Scale - English Miles

MAP 5

THE UNITED KINGDOM OF SAUL, DAVID AND SOLOMON

Scale — English Miles

NOTE
For fuller details see Map of the
Kingdoms of Judah and Israel

MAP 6

MAP 7

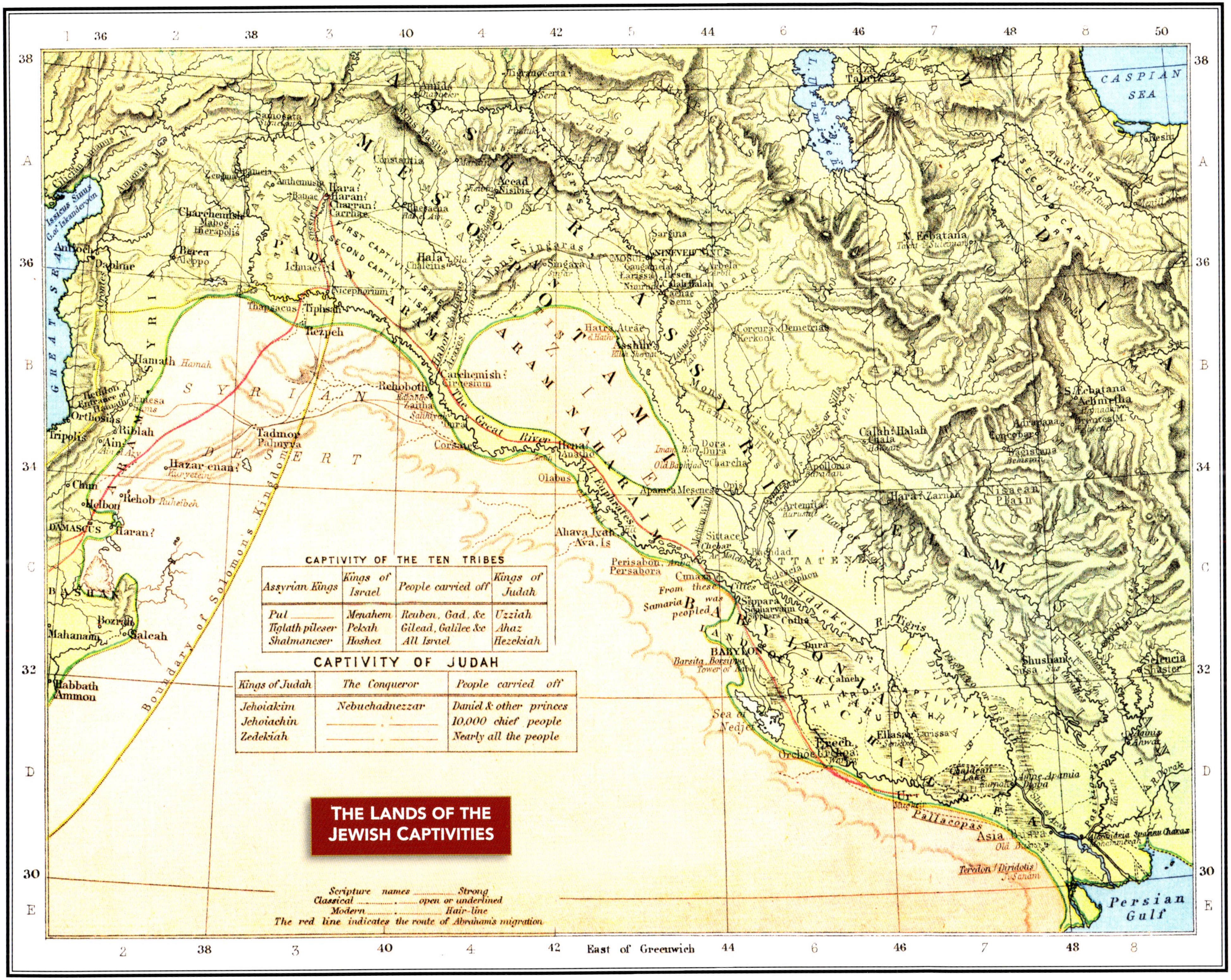

THE LANDS OF THE JEWISH CAPTIVITIES

CAPTIVITY OF THE TEN TRIBES

Assyrian Kings	Kings of Israel	People carried off	Kings of Judah
Pul	Menahem	Reuben, Gad, &c	Uzziah
Tiglath-pileser	Pekah	Gilead, Galilee &c	Ahaz
Shalmaneser	Hoshea	All Israel	Hezekiah

CAPTIVITY OF JUDAH

Kings of Judah	The Conqueror	People carried off
Jehoiakim	Nebuchadnezzar	Daniel & other princes
Jehoiachin		10,000 chief people
Zedekiah		Nearly all the people

Scripture names .... Strong
Classical .... open or underlined
Modern .... Hair-line
The red line indicates the route of Abraham's migration.

CASPIAN SEA

L. Urumiah

PERSIAN GULF

East of Greenwich

MEDIA

ASSYRIA

MESOPOTAMIA

ARAM NAHARAIM

SYRIA

BABYLONIA

PADAN ARAM

SYRIAN DESERT

GREAT SEA

Boundary of Solomon's Kingdom

MAP 8

PALESTINE AT THE TIME OF CHRIST

Scale

English | 10 | 20 Miles

Sidon

Sarepta

Tyre

Ptolemais

DAMASCUS

SYRIA

TETRARCHY ABILENE OF LYSANIAS

Mt Hermon

CÆSAREA PHILIPPI

TETRARCHY

TRACHONITIS

OF

PHŒNICE

UPPER GALILEE

Chorazin Bethsaida
Capernaum
Bethsaida

Magdala
Dalmanutha
Cana TIBERIAS

Gergesenes
Gergesa
SEA OF GALILEE

GAULANITIS

PHILIP

BATANÆA

Nazareth
Mt Tabor
LOWER
Nain

GALILEE

Gadara
Gadara

DECAPOLIS

Salim
Ænon

CAESAREA

SAMARIA
Jacob's Well Sychar

Antipatris

Joppa

Arimathaea

Lydda

Ephraim

Beth-abara

Ford of Jordan, where first baptised

Jericho

The Wilderness
Mt of Olives

Emmaus

Azotus

Bethany
JERUSALEM
Cedron
Bethlehem

Gaza

ROMAN PROVINCE OF JUDÆA

TETRARCHY

Wilderness of Judæa

THE SALT SEA

IDUMÆA

ARABIA

TETRARCHY OF ANTIPAS BEYOND JORDAN

PERÆA

East from Greenwich

MAP 9

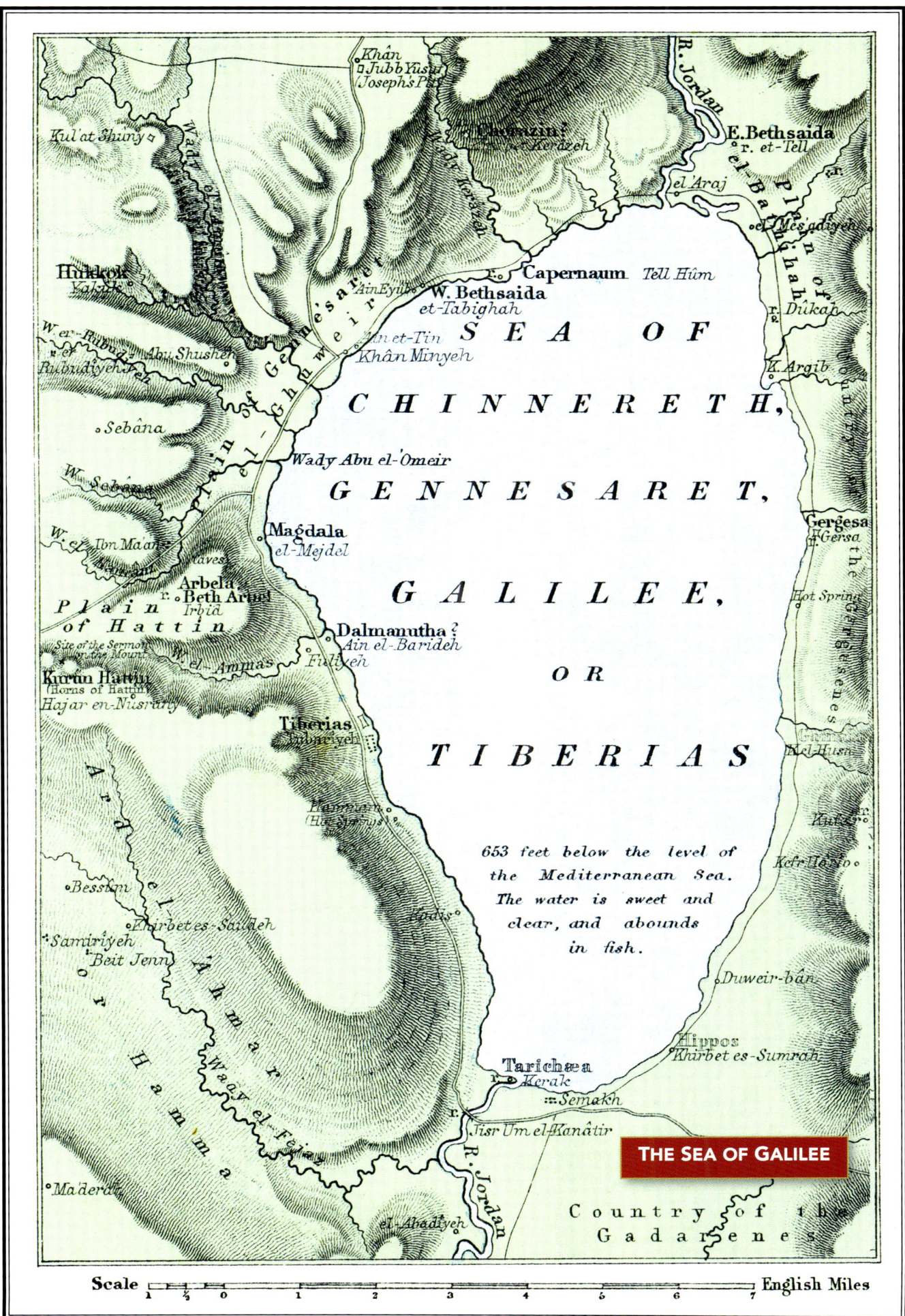

THE SEA OF GALILEE

MAP 10

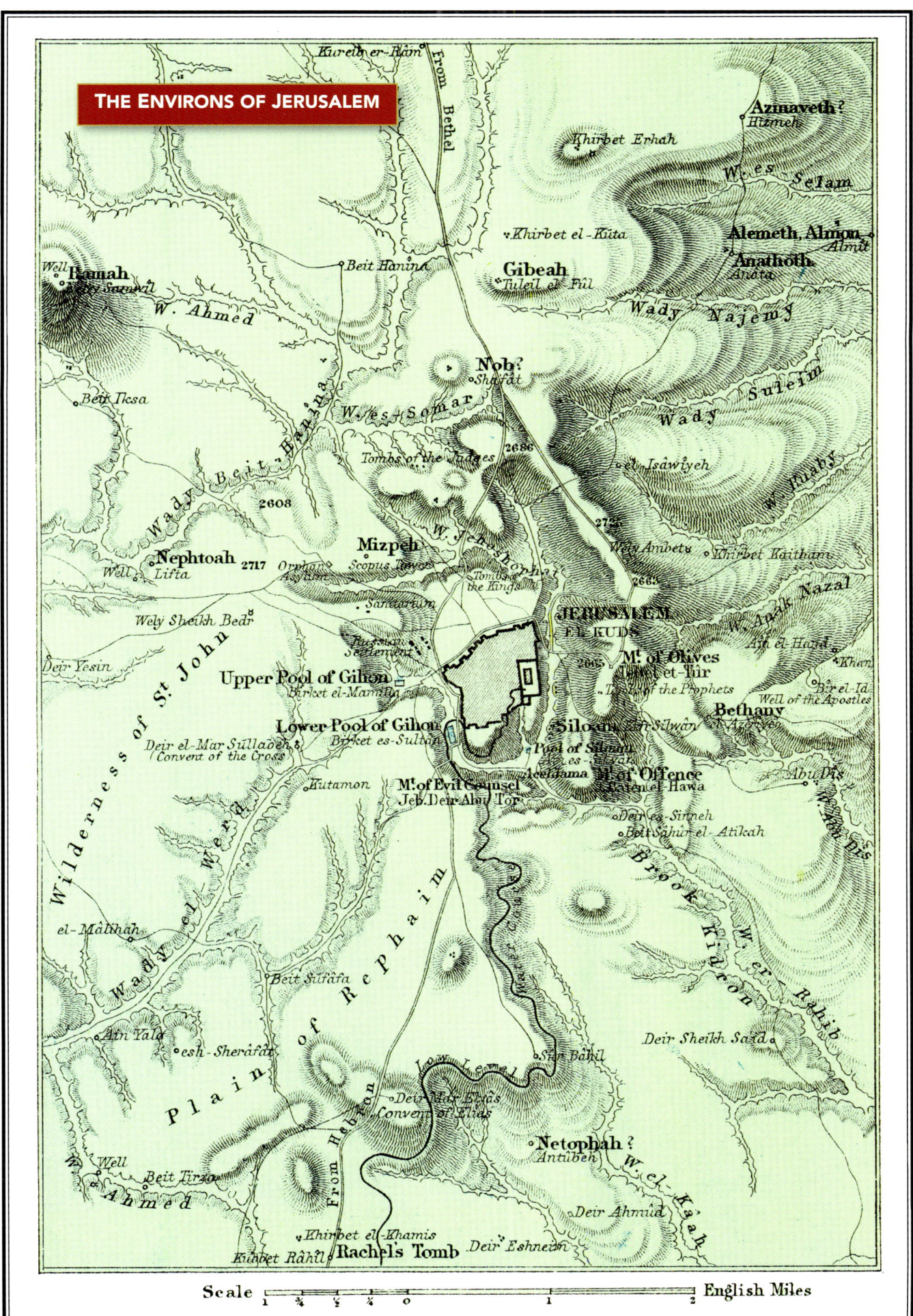

THE ENVIRONS OF JERUSALEM

Kureit er-Rám
From Bethel
Azmaveth?
Hizmeh
Khirbet Erhah
W. es Selam
Khirbet el-Kúta
Alemeth, Almon
Almit
Anathoth.
Gibeah
Anata
Beit Hanina
Tuleil el-Fûl
Wady Najewy
Hamah
Neby Samwil
Well
W. Ahmed
Beit Iksa
Nob?
Sha'fat
W. es Somar
Wady Suleim
el-Isâwîyeh
W. Habr
Tombs of the Judges
2686
2608
Mizpeh
2724
Wely Ambeta
Khirbet Kaitham
Nephtoah
2717
Scopus Tower
266
Lifta
Well
Orphan
Tombs
the Kings
Asylum
Samaritan
JERUSALEM
EL KUDS
W. Arak Nazal
Wely Sheikh Bedr
Ain el-Haud
Deir Yesin
Russian
Settlement
2685
Mt of Olives
Khan
Birket el-Mamilla
Tombs of the Prophets
Bir el-Id
Upper Pool of Gihon
Well of the Apostles
Bethany
Deir el-Mar Sûlladeh &
Convent of the Cross
Lower Pool of Gihon
Birket es-Sultan
Siloam
Kerbet-Tûr
Kefr Silwân
el-Azariyeh
Pool of Siloam
Wilderness of St John
Kutamon
Aceldama
Mt of Offence
Batn el-Hawa
Abu Dis
Mt of Evil Counsel
Jeb. Deir Abu Tor
Deir es-Sinneh
Beit Sahûr el-Atikah
Brook Kidron
W. er Rahib
el-Malhah
Plain of Rephaim
Water Course
Wady el Werd
W. Ahmed
Deir Sheikh Said
Ain Yalo
esh-Sherâfât
Beit Sufâfa
Sûr Bahil
Low Level
Deir Mar Elias
Convent of Elias
Well
Beit Tirza
From Hebron
Netophah?
Antûbeh
W. el-Kaab
Deir Ahmûd
Khirbet el-Khamis
Khirbet Râhil
Rachel's Tomb
Deir Eshneim

Scale 1 ¾ ½ ¼ 0 1 2 English Miles

MAP 11

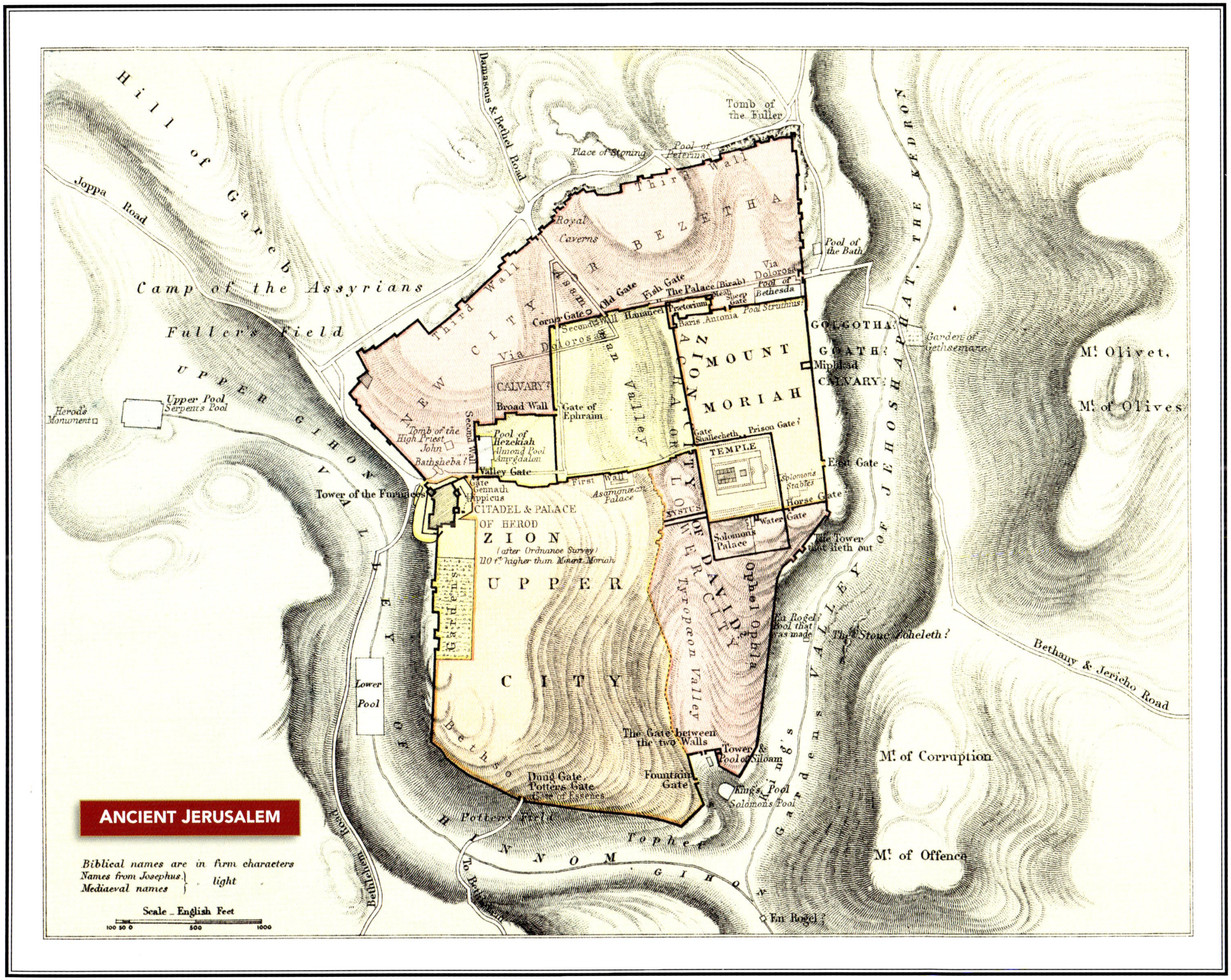

MAP 12

ANCIENT JERUSALEM

Mt. Olivet.

Mt. of Olives.

Bethany & Jericho Road

Mt. of Corruption

Mt. of Offence

THE KEDRON

VALLEY OF JEHOSHAPHAT

Garden of Gethsemane

The Stone Zoheleth?

En Rogel?

Gihon

Gardens

Tomb of the Fuller

Pool of the Baths

GOLGOTHA?

GATH

CALVARY

MOUNT MORIAH

East Gate?

Tower where Joab fleeth out

Pool of Siloam

Aenon Pool

Solomon's Pool

Hill of Bezetha

TEMPLE

ACRA, OR LOWER CITY OF DAVID

Ophel Ophla

Antonia

Prison Gate?

Water Gate?

Solomon's Palace

THIRD WALL

Place of Stoning?

Via Dolorosa

Pool of Bethesda

The Sheep

Tyropoeon Valley

Tower & Pool of Siloam

Royal Caverns

Old Gate

Fish Gate

Hananeel

Turris

Corner Gate

Second Wall

Hill

Gate Sabbath

The Palace Bridge?

Xystus

BEZETHA OR NEW CITY

Asmonean Valley

TYROPOEON OR CHEESEMAKERS VALLEY

UPPER CITY

The Gate between the two Walls

Valley

Gate of Ephraim

Asmonean Palace

First Wall

ZION

Fountain Gate

CALVARY

Broad Wall

Via Dolorosa

Pool of Hezekiah

Almond Pool

Amygdalon

CITADEL & PALACE OF HEROD

Dung Gate

Potters' Gate

Gennath

Hippicus

Phasaelus

(after Ordnance Survey)

110 ft higher than Mount Moriah

UPPER CITY

Gardens

Second Wall

Valley Gate

Tomb of the High Priest John?

Bathsheba?

To Bethlehem

Tower of the Furnaces?

Hill of Gareb or Assyrians

Camp of the Assyrians

Fullers Field

UPPER GIHON

VALLEY OF HINNOM

Bezetha

Aceldama

Lower Pool

Bethlehem Road

Damascus & Bethel Road

Joppa Road

Upper Pool Serpent's Pool

Herod's Monument

ANCIENT JERUSALEM

Biblical names are in firm characters
Names from Josephus } light
Mediaeval names

Scale – English Feet

100 50 0   500   1000

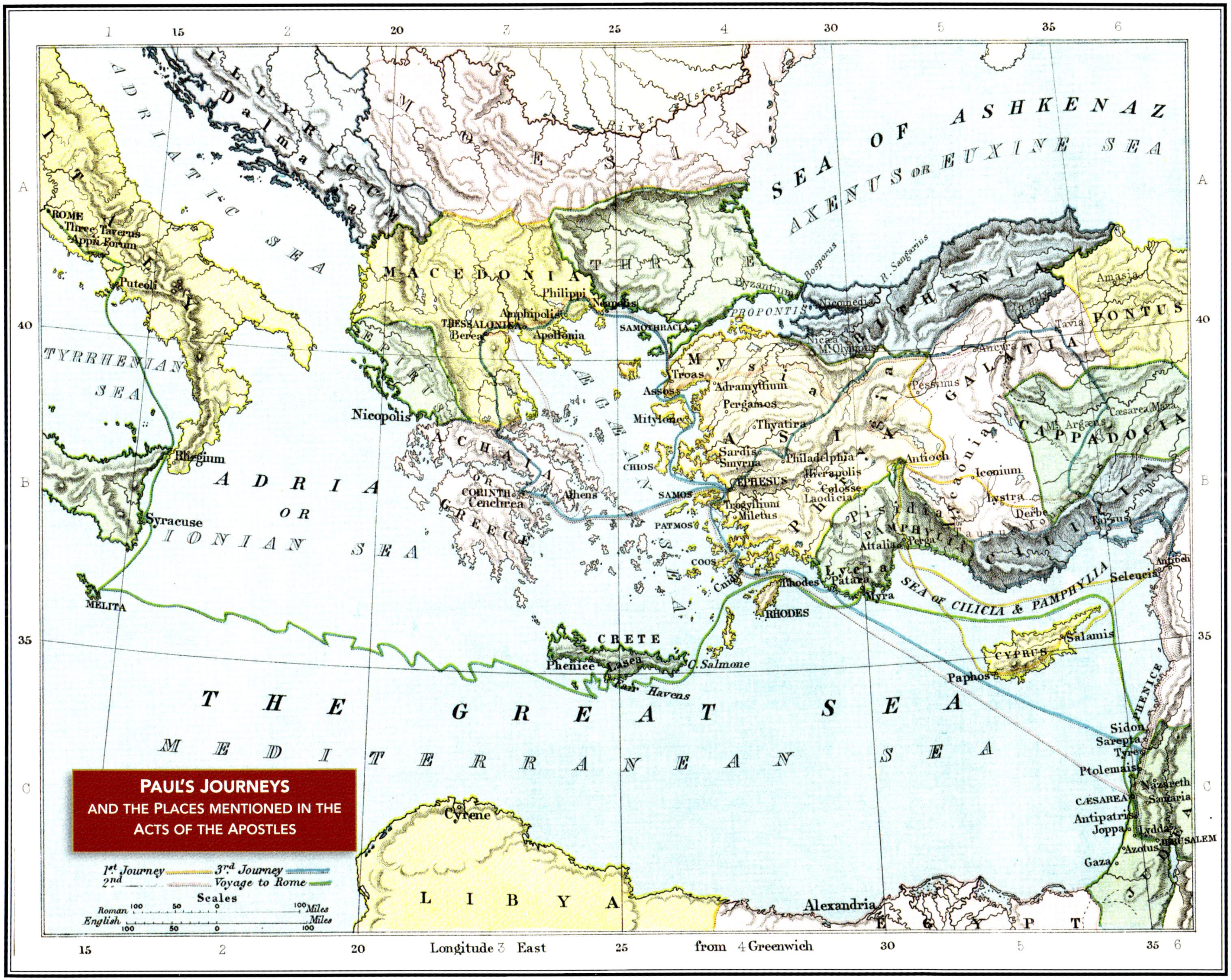
PAUL'S JOURNEYS
AND THE PLACES MENTIONED IN THE ACTS OF THE APOSTLES
1st Journey
2nd
3rd Journey
Voyage to Rome
Scales
Roman 100 50 0 100 Miles
English 100 50 0 100 Miles
SEA OF ASHKENAZ
AXENUS OR EUXINE SEA
ADRIATIC SEA
TYRRHENIAN SEA
ADRIA OR IONIAN SEA
THE GREAT SEA
MEDITERRANEAN SEA
SEA OF CILICIA & PAMPHYLIA
ITALY
ILLYRICUM
Dalmatia
MOESIA
MACEDONIA
THRACE
EPIRUS
ACHAIA OR GREECE
BITHYNIA
PONTUS
GALATIA
CAPPADOCIA
CILICIA
Mysia
ASIA
Phrygia
Pisidia
Lycaonia
PAMPHYLIA
Lycia
CRETE
CYPRUS
PHENICE
LIBYA
EGYPT
JUDÆA
ROME
Three Taverns
Appii Forum
Puteoli
Rhegium
Syracuse
MELITA
Nicopolis
THESSALONICA
Berea
Amphipolis
Apollonia
Philippi
Neapolis
SAMOTHRACIA
Byzantium
PROPONTIS
Bosporus
R. Sangarius
Nicomedia
Nicæa
M. Olympus
CORINTH
Cenchrea
Athens
Troas
Assos
Mitylene
CHIOS
SAMOS
PATMOS
COOS
Cnidus
Rhodes
RHODES
Adramyttium
Pergamos
Thyatira
Sardis
Smyrna
EPHESUS
Trogyllium
Miletus
Philadelphia
Hierapolis
Colosse
Laodicia
Antioch
Iconium
Lystra
Derbe
Tarsus
Attalia
Perga
Patara
Myra
Pessinus
Ancyra
Tavia
Amasia
Cæsarea Mazaca
M. Argæus
Seleucia
Antioch
Salamis
Paphos
C. Salmone
Phenice
Lasea
Fair Havens
Cyrene
Alexandria
Sidon
Sarepta
Tyre
Ptolemais
Nazareth
Samaria
CÆSAREA
Antipatris
Joppa
Lydda
JERUSALEM
Azotus
Gaza
Longitude East from Greenwich

MAP 13

THE DISTRIBUTION OF NATIONS AFTER THE DELUGE
MAP 1

This map is to illustrates the dispersion of the children of Noah, 'after their families, after their tongues, in their lands, after their nations,' as described in the tenth chapter of Genesis, and incorporated, with some slight alterations, in the genealogies of the First Book of Chronicles. This information is obviously arranged on a genealogical basis, and it gives in many instances the names of the founders of nations. But in other instances, the names of peoples are given which appear to be derived, not from their founders, but from the designations of the lands which they occupied. As a general rule, those names which end in 'im' are plural, denoting races, not individual persons.

A considerable proportion of the names in Genesis 10 became current names in Hebrew geography, as it is represented in the later books of the Old Testament. We have thus in many cases a safe guide as to the general positions of the regions to which they belong, though the areas to which they were applied were often widely extended in later times. Thus Kittim became a general name for the maritime lands of the west, and Magog for the regions of Northern Asia. It should be observed that each name is placed in this map in the spot to which it appears, according to such evidence as exists, to have first belonged, and with which it was probably identified in the mind of the author of Genesis 10, without regard to the subsequent extension of its area. The following notes chiefly relate to the names of most importance, and to those particulars that throw light on their geographical positions.

The Sons of Japheth (Genesis 10:2)
Gomer is almost universally regarded as the father of the Cimmerians, or Gomerians, who first appear in history on the north shore of the Euxine Sea. Their name long remained there in the designations – the Cimmerian Bosporus, the Cimmerian Mount and the Cimmerian Walls – and a trace of them still survives in the name Crimea. They must thus have been in Asia Minor, in the close neighbourhood of Armenia, when Ezekiel (38:6) wrote of them as associated with Togarmah (the Armenians) in the confederacy under Gog, the chief of Magog (the Scythians), which was to threaten the peace of Israel after the return from the captivity, but was to suffer defeat. It has been conjectured with much probability that the Celtic nations are descended from Cimmerians who migrated to the West.

Magog is mentioned in Ezekiel 38:2, 39:6. The name has been universally understood to denote the Scythians, who in the time of Ezekiel had spread to the westward, and driven out the Cimmerians. The term Magog was probably afterwards applied to all who dwelt beyond the Caucasus, and the Caspian and Euxine Seas. The word Goy appears to have been a title of the ruler of Magog, the head of a confederation comprising Gomer, Togarmah, Meshech and Tubal formed after the captivity.

Madai is the regular name for the Medes, while Javan appears to have been taken for the Greek race.

The Tower of Babel (Genesis 11:8–9)

Tubal is almost always associated with Meshech. It appears that the Alexandrian translators did not connect the names with any peoples known to the Greeks and Romans. Josephus supposes Tubal to have been the father of the Iberians, and Meshech the father of the Cappadocians.

The Sons of Gomer (Genesis 10:3)
Ashkenaz is noticed only in the passages of Genesis and in Jeremiah 49:27, where the prophet mentions together 'the kingdoms of Ararat, Minni, and Ashkenaz'.

The Sons of Javan (Genesis 10:4)
Elishah – 'The Isles of Elishah' are spoken of by Ezekiel (27:7) as supplying the famous purple dye. Javan and Elishah represent two of the great divisions of the Greek race.

Tarshish, in some places, Tharshish – Its locality is very doubtful. There is no other ground for connecting it with Tarsus in Cilicia than the similarity of the names, and the unsupported statement of Josephus that the Cilicians were formerly called Tharsi. The earliest legends make the Cilician Tarsus to have been a Greek colony, but they do not in any way account for the name, which was no doubt given to it in very ancient times, whether it was derived from the son of Javan or not.

Kittim, elsewhere Chittin – Josephus states that the ancient name of Cyprus was Chetima. Kitium was well known as the name of one of its cities. Josephus also says that the Hebrews in later times extended the name Chittim to most of the islands and sea coasts that were known to them; and this is confirmed in several passages of the Old Testament.

The Sons Of Ham (Genesis 10:6.)
Canaan, the youngest son of Ham, divided the 'Land of Canaan' among his eleven sons, whose descendants resided there for upwards of seven centuries, and founded numerous republics and kingdoms.

Cush was the ordinary name for Ethiopia, and is so rendered in the Bible, except in Genesis 10 and Isaiah 11:11. The basin of the Nile south of Egypt is generally called Cush in Egyptian monuments.

Mizraim was the usual name for Egypt. The Hebrew word is in the dual form, and seems to denote the two Egypts, i.e., Upper and Lower; or, as is more probable, East and West, as divided by the Nile.

The Children of Shem (Genesis 10:21-22)
Elam was originally the name of the province of Persia, of which Susa was the capital (Daniel 8:2; Ezra 4:9). The name appears to have been applied to the whole of Persia in later times (Isaiah 11:11, 21:2; Ezekiel 32:24).

Asshur was used strictly as the name of Assyria; but it sometimes included Babylonia with the land of the Chaldees.

Arphaxad appears to be recognized as the father of the Chaldees (in Genesis 11, compare verse 12 with verse 28). But the situation of the country to which his name was first applied is doubtful.

Aram was the name of Syria, but more especially of the high land of Lebanon. The original word is preserved in Numbers 23:7; elsewhere it is rendered as Syria.

The Nations Of Canaan (Genesis 10:15-19)

The Hittites, the children of Heth, must have been in the neighbourhood of Hebron (then Kirjath-Arba) when Abraham purchased from them the cave of Machpelah (Genesis 23:3–9).

The Jebusites appear to have inhabited the site of Jerusalem in the time of Joshua (Joshua 15:8).

The Amorites occupied Hazezon-Tamar, i.e., Engedi) when Abraham fought the battle with the Kings (Genesis 14:7).

The Hivites inhabited Shechem in the time of Jacob (Genesis 34:2) and were masters of Gibeon in the time of Joshua (Joshua 9:7). It has been conjectured that the original seat of the Hivites is indicated in the expression in Joshua 11:3, 'The Hivite under Mount Hermon', and that those who settled in Gibeon and the neighbouring cities were a colony from that place

THE GENTILE COUNTRIES AND NATIONS OF THE OLD TESTAMENT
MAP 2

A large proportion of the names in this map occur in the tenth chapter of Genesis and may be found in the first map. But many of these names here occupy different, and in most instances, more extended areas. The present map shows as accurately as possible the place identified with each name by the Hebrews, when the commerce of the kings and their trade with the Phoenicians had increased their geographical knowledge. In the first map, on the other hand, the name is placed where, according to available information, it appears to have been applied in the earliest ages.

It should be observed that the Bible is by no means consistent in the treatment of geographical names. In some cases the Hebrew name is retained, while in others a classical or a modern name is substituted for it.

Arabia is the Greek form of the native name of which the Hebrew form first occurs in the Bible in the time of Solomon. (1 Kings 10:15.) The name in the Old Testament does not denote the whole of the vast peninsula now known as Arabia, but only the portion of it that lay immediately south and east of the Holy Land, called in earlier times 'the East Country'. (Genesis 25:6, 39:1). It was in all probability only coextensive with the region of the Ishmaelites.

Armenia, the Greek name for Ararat, was peopled by the sons of Togarmah. The name Ararat appears strictly to belong to the central province of Armenia: this was without doubt the Ararat of Genesis, (7:4).

Asshur, (Numbers 24:22) in the Prophets and Historical Books, denotes the Assyrian Empire.

Chaldaea, in its stricter sense, appears to be the great alluvial plain at the head of the Persian Gulf, containing the confluence of the Tigris and the Euphrates. In later times it seems to have been applied to the whole of Babylonia.

Cush – Ethiopia. The name Cush is kept in our version only in the text of Genesis 10 and in Isaiah 11:11; Ethiopia is used in all other places.

Dedan, mentioned in connection with Tema and Buz in Jeremiah 25:23, and with Edom and Teman in Jeremiah 49:7, 8, etc., appears to have been the tribe of Dedan, the grandson of Abraham and Keturah (Genesis 25:3). It was probably this pastoral tribe that supplied the Tyrians with 'precious cloths', or rugs, for chariots (Ezekiel 32:20).

Dedan or Dedanim (Cushite) on the shore of the Persian Gulf. This people became famous as traders in ivory and ebony, conveying the produce of India to the west (Ezekiel 27:15). The Cushite is associated with maritime nations and used to supply Tyre with merchandise that must necessarily have been brought by sea. The Shemite Dedan, on the other hand, is associated with his pastoral brethren (in Jeremiah 25:23, 49:8), and the 'precious cloths 'were probably made from the skins or wool of his flock' (Ezekiel 27:20).

Dumah seems to have been the region of an Ishmaelite tribe that took its name from a son of Ishmael (Genesis 25:14). It would seem, from Isaiah 21:11, to have been connected with Seir (Edom).

Edom – Seir – Idumaea – The name of Seir was applied to the mountainous region originally inhabited by the Horites (Genesis 14:6; 36:20,22). The Horites were succeeded by the children of Esau, and from him the land was generally called Edom. (Genesis 25:30; 32:3; 36:9,16; Deuteronomy 4, etc.). Elath and Ezion-geber were, in the time of its prosperity, its seaports (1 Kings 9:26, etc.), but they fell into the hands of Solomon and his successors for a time and afterwards into those of the Syrians.

Kedar was the second son of Ishmael (Genesis 25:13). The tribe that bore his name were skilful archers (Isaiah 21:17). They seem to have been in the time of the Prophets the most powerful of the nomads of Arabia.

Ramah was a market of the Tyrians for spices, gems, etc.

Seba, the Cushite tribe, appears to have become the chief trading people of the southwest coast of the Red Sea and is coupled with Sheba as the trading people of the other side of the Sea in Psalms 72:10.

Sheba, originally the seat of a single Joktanite tribe (Genesis 10:28) appears to have expanded into the important kingdom that existed in the time of King Solomon (I Kings 10:1; Isaiah 40:6, Jeremiah 6:20). 'The gold of Sheba' had become a common phrase, interchangeable, it would seem, with 'the gold of Ophir'.

Syria is the Greek name for the country that included what the Hebrews call Aram, which in its stricter sense probably included only the highlands of Libanus and Antililanus; but Aram was used also for the whole of Syria.

Tharshish, or Tarshish. The name appears to denote the great western region of commerce that was known to the Hebrews, while Ophir, Sheba, and Seba denote the eastern and southern commercial regions on the Asiatic and African coasts (Psalms 72:10, etc.).

Zoan was the ancient capital of Lower Egypt, the maritime or delta region, which also contained Migdol and Taphenes.

THE EXODUS
MAP 3

The route taken by the Israelites may be conveniently divided into four portions:

1. From Rameses to the Red Sea.
2. From the Red Sea to Sinai.
3. From Sinai to Kadesh-barnea.
4. From Kadesh-barnea to the Plains of Moab.

The Land of Goshen may strictly be called some of the 'best of the land' of Egypt. This region was not only of great importance on account of its fertility, but also on account of its position in reference to commerce and traffic of all kinds. The most available lines of intercourse between the Nile and the western arm of the Red Sea lay through it, as well as the best direct line from the Red Sea to the Mediterranean. On this account, from the earliest times since Egypt became a great nation, the country appears to have been intersected by canals, and the towns spoken of in the history of the Exodus were essentially connected with the canal traffic.

Zoan – There seems no good reason to doubt that the residence of the Egyptian court, when Moses was negotiating for the liberation of the Israelites, was at Zoan, the old royal city of the delta. (See Numbers 13:22; Isaiah 19:11,13, 30:4.)

The waters of the Red Sea close upon the pursuing Egyptians

From Rameses to the Red Sea (Exodus 12:37, 13:20, 45:2,9 and Numbers 13:5-8)

Various opinions have been held regarding the situation of Rameses, the city from where the Israelites commenced their march. It was one of the 'treasure cities' which the Israelites had built, or rather restored, for Pharaoh (Exodus 1:11), and it must have been the capital of Goshen (Genesis 45:12, 47:11).

Succoth, the place of the first encampment,

Gathering manna

was probably at a very short distance from Rameses. The first movement of a vast mixed host of men, women, and children would hardly have taken place without a careful review of their equipment for the march, and such a review may have been made at Succoth.

The Red Sea – It has been generally supposed that the Israelites crossed the sea at the narrow strait of Suez where the distance from one shore to the other is 3,450 feet, or about two-thirds of a mile. God, it is said, caused the sea to go (or to flow out) by a strong east wind. The miracle, therefore, could possibly be represented as a miraculous adaptation of the laws of nature to produce a required result. A strong northeasterly wind acting here upon the ebb-tide would necessarily have the effect of driving out the waters from the small arm of the sea that runs up by Suez, and also from the end of the gulf itself, leaving the shallower portions dry, while the more northern part of the arm, which was anciently broad and deep, would still remain covered with water. Thus the waters would be divided, and be a wall (or defence) to the Israelites on the right hand and on the left.'

From the Red Sea to Sinai (Exodus 15:22 to 19:1, Numbers 33:8-15)

From the Red Sea they advanced to the Wilderness of Sin, where the supply of manna commenced (Exodus 16:4).

From the Wilderness of Sin there are three possible routes to the place where the Law was given; the positions which have been given to the intermediate stations – Dophkah, Alush and Rephidim – have varied accordingly.

But essentially connected with the inquiry regarding the route is the great question in the topography of the Sinai peninsula: which is the true Sinai, the summit from which the voice of God gave the Law to Moses? There are four heights to which this distinguished honour has been, with more or less confidence, ascribed by different writers. The sacred narrative appears to require that there should be a mountain, or cliff, with a plain in front of it sufficiently large for the encampment of a great host. There are at least three summits in the group that are said to answer convincingly to these conditions.

Mount Sinai

There is a quadrangular mass of tableland near the middle of the entire group of mountains, the length of which from northwest to southeast is about five miles, and the width about two. It is bounded at the sides by narrow ravines. At each end it rises into a summit, which precipitously slopes down to a plain of considerable extent. It is between these two summits that the opinions of the greater number of critics are divided. The one which has the support of local tradition is at the south extremity of the tableland. It is called by the Arabs Jebel Mûsa (i.e., 'the Mountain of Moses'). Its height above the sea is about 7,000 feet, and above the plain at its foot, 2,000 feet.

From Sinai to Kadesh-barnea (Numbers 10:33, 11:3,34,35, 12:16, 13:26, 20:1 and 33:16–18)

From this point the route of the Israelites is of increasing importance

Moses strikes the rock with his staff

owing to the more fragmentary character of the historical narrative. Assuming that the encampment at Kadesh-barnea was the same as that spoken of as the encampment at Rithmah in Numbers 33:18, there were but two stations between it and the foot of Mount Sinai. The first of these, Kibroth-Hattaavait, evidently appears to be the same as Taberah (Numbers 11; compare verses 3 and 34), and was three days' journey from Sinai (Numbers 10:33).

Numbers 12:16 states that they 'removed from Hazeroth, and pitched in the wilderness of Paran'. It was from this encampment 'in the wilderness of Paran' that the twelve spies were sent (Numbers 13:3), and they 'returned unto the wilderness of Paran, to Kadesh' (Numbers 13:26). They are said (Numbers 13:21) to have 'searched the land from the Wilderness of Zin unto Rehob'. In Numbers 32:8 and Deuteronomy 11:23 it is stated that the spies were sent from Kadesh-barnea.

Kadesh was a city (Numbers 20:16) situated in the Wilderness of Zin, which the Israelites visited twice: first,

The spies return

Moses receives the Law at Mount Sinai

when they entered the Wilderness of Zin from Hazeroth, soon after leaving Sinai in the second year of their migrations; and secondly, after extending their journeys to Ezion-geber, (Numbers 33:35) in or about the fortieth year (Numbers 33:38) when Miriam died and Moses struck the rock, and when the King of Edorn refused them a passage through his territory.

From Kadesh-barnea to the Plains of Moab

When the Israelites left Kadesh the first time, they appear to have passed down the Arabah to Ezion-geber and to have halted at sixteen stations (Numbers 33:20–35). From Ezion-geber (Numbers 33:35) the host appears to have returned up the Arabah to Kadesh-barnea. On their second departure from Kadesh, they came to Mount Hor and journeyed from there 'by the way of the Red Sea, to compass the land of Edom' (Numbers 21:4). On this occasion they must have passed down the Arabah a second time, probably to Elath (Deuteronomy 2:8) and gone round the region of Mount Seir. The sites of the stations until they came to the brook Zered are wholly uncertain. Kadesh and the brook Zered, or Zared, were regarded as the two great points in the passage of the Israelites through the wilderness from Sinai to the Promised Land. Deuteronomy 2:13,14.

Moses sees the Promised Land from the top of Mount Nebo

THE HOLY LAND AS ALLOTTED TO THE TWELVE TRIBES

MAP 5

The West Side of the Jordan

The great natural features of the land of Israel connect themselves geographically with the regions on the north rather than with those on the south. The double range of heights that skirts the east coast of the Mediterranean is interrupted for a short space at the foot of Mount Hermon by a plain that slopes towards the sea and is traversed by the upper stream of the River Jordan and the lower stream of the Litany, the ancient Leontes. From this plain a depressed strip, about ten miles wide, extends southwards between two ranges of heights, with gradually increasing depth, and through this strip the Jordan makes its way. The highlands on the west extend for 180 miles, with an average breadth of eighteen miles, down to the wilderness, with which they are geologically connected.

The South Country, or Negeb, was the ordinary designation of a well defined region. The sense in the Bible is made obscure owing to the name being rendered vaguely 'the south', or incorrectly as 'the way southward' (Genesis 12:1,3, Numbers 13:17,22, 21;1, 34:4, etc.), and many writers on the geography of the Bible have fallen into similar confusion. The 29 cities of the Negeb are named in Joshua 15:21–32, where they are distinguished from the cities of the other natural divisions originally allotted to Judah.

The Wilderness of Judah skirted the northern half of the west coast of the Dead Sea. The six cities that it contained are enumerated in Joshua 15:61–2. The desolation that marks it nearly throughout the year is but very slightly relieved here and there by a spot of scanty vegetation in the early summer.

Joshua leads the Hebrews cross the River Jordan

The Hills, the Mountain, and the Mountains, are the names by which the Hill Country, the portion of the tableland extending from the foot of Lebanon southward to the Wilderness, is called. The Hittites, the Jebusites and the Amorites are named as the old inhabitants of the Hill Country (Numbers 13:29). A list of the cities in the southern part, the portion awarded to the tribe of Judah, is given in Joshua 15:48–60.

The Arabah, the sunken strip reaching from the foot of Hermon to the Gulf of Akabah, has been pronounced to be the most remarkable depression on the face of the earth. The River Jordan, taking its rise in the slopes of Hermon, spreads out in the waters of Merom at the height of 126 feet above the sea level, and after about ten miles of rapid descent it enters the sea at Chinnereth, the surface of which is 650 feet below sea level.

The East Side of the Jordan

The range of heights on the east side of the Arabah are of a more decidedly mountainous character than the Hill Country of the Land of Canaan. Mount Seir, or 'the land of Seir' (Genesis 32:3 and 36:30), the ancient abode of the children of Esau, is a rugged ridge of sandstone, rising to a height of 4,800 feet, with deep clefts opening towards the Arabah. North of Mount Seir, the mountainous tableland of Moab skirts the Dead Sea as far as those verdant upland pastures and flourishing forests of Gilead and Bashan, which tempted the tribes of Reuben and Gad, with half the tribe of Manasseh, to take up their abode on the east side of Jordan (Numbers 32:6, Deuteronomy 32:14, Psalms 22:12, Isaiah 2:13, Ezekiel 37:1, 39:18 and Amos 4:1.). The Hills of Bashan attain the height of 6,400 feet, and their western drainage waters the plain of the Hauran, of which the elevation exceeds 2,500 feet.

The Division of the Holy Land

The settlement of the Tribes east of the Jordan – Reuben, Gad, and half the Tribe of Manasseh – is related in Numbers 32:1–42. These tribes appear to have been richer than their brethren in terms of flocks and herds. They were attracted by the rich pastures of Gilead and Bashan and applied to Moses for the possession of them. Their request was granted on condition of their lending help to the other tribes to subdue the land on the west side of the river. The formal allotment of the transjordanic region by Moses is described in Joshua 13:8–32. It was not until the old age of Joshua that the remaining nine tribes and a half received their portions between the river and the sea (Joshua 13:1–7).

The territory apportioned to Judah is described in Joshua 15:1–12, and its cities are enumerated in verses 21–62. But it afterwards appeared that the region was larger than the tribe required, and a portion of it was removed for Simeon, which thus became the frontier tribe of the South (Joshua 19:1–9).

The portion of Ephraim, and that of the half tribe of Manasseh, are described in Joshua 16 and 17. When the allotment of Judah, Ephraim and Manasseh were determined, the Tabernacle was solemnly set up at Shiloh, in the portion allotted to Ephraim, as a recognition of the power of the house of Joseph.

An interval appears now to have elapsed before the places were appointed for the other seven tribes (Joshua 18:2). Their limits are given in Joshua 18:11 and 19:48. The territory allotted to Dan proved to be too small for the whole tribe, and a portion of the Danites migrated to the north and conquered the district of Leshem, or Laish, the name of which they changed to Dan (Joshua 19:47).

It should be noted that there were certain towns belonging to Ephraim situated within the borders of Manasseh (Joshua 16:9 and 17:9) and some belonging to Manasseh within the borders of Issachar and Asher (Joshua 17:11).

THE UNITED KINGDOM OF SAUL, DAVID AND SOLOMON
MAP 6

By David's victories over the Philistines, the Edomites, the Moabites and the nations of Syria, the territory of the Hebrews was extended to its utmost limits (II Samuel 8:1–15). The divine promise made to Abraham was now fulfilled almost to the letter: 'Unto thy seed have I given this land, from the river of Egypt unto the great river, the river Euphrates' (Genesis 15:18). The organization of this region by Solomon is described in I Kings 4:1–28 and 9:17–23. Solomon became possessed of Ezion-geber and Elath, the seaports on the Red Sea, owing to the victories of David over the Edomites. This enabled him to carry on trade with the shores of the Indian Ocean (I Kings 9:26 and II Chronicles 8:17,18, etc.), and the traffic in their rich products appears to have been very lucrative. It was, apparently, with a view to land traffic with the east that he built Tadmor in the desert, which was afterwards called by the Greeks Palmyra (II Chronicles 8:4).

God makes his promise to Abraham

David the shepherd boy

David annointed king

Solomon greets the Queen of Sheba

Solomon's kingdom becomes a very wealthy nation with trade links far and wide

According to the words of Ahijah the prophet, taken literally, one tribe only – that of Judah – was to be reserved for the House of David, while ten were to take part with Jeroboam (I Kings 11:35,36.) The terms of the prophecy may have had reference to the commencement of David's reign, when he was 'annointed king over the House of Judah' (II Samuel 2:4–11), and when Abner maintained for two years the authority of Ishbosheth 'over Gilead, and over the Ashurites' (perhaps the Asherites, i.e., the Israelites dwelling north of Jezreel, called by the name of Asher, the chief tribe) 'and over Jezreel, and over Ephraim, and over Benjamin, and over all Israel' (II Samuel 2:9). But it appears that the whole, or nearly the whole, of Benjamin, as well as Simeon and southern Dan, immediately submitted to Rehoboam and continued to form parts of the Kingdom of Judah. It is not possible to mark the limits of the two kingdoms with exactness, as conflicts and exchanges often occurred in the border land. It appears that Bethel, Jericho and other towns passed over from one kingdom to the other probably more than once (II Chronicles 13, 19; 15:8, 17:2 and I Kings 16:34).

Jeroboam at first made Shechem his capital (I Kings 12:25), but afterwards Tirzah (I Kings 16:17), which continued to be the residence of the kings of Israel until Omri built

Rehoboam divides the kingdom

Elijah on Mount Carmel

Samaria (I Kings 15:21,33 and 16:8,15,23,24).

Galilee (Joshua 20:7 and I Kings 9:11) was originally the name of a district around the city of Kedesh, containing the twenty cities that Solomon gave to Hiram as a payment for the timber sent to Jerusalem for his grand construction projects. The name Cabul, (i.e., 'the dirty place') at first the name of one of the twenty cities, appears according to Josephus to have been applied to this district by Hiram in the way of a pun. The name Galilee was subsequently extended over what seems to have been called the land of the Ashurites (Asher).

The fall of Samaria

The fall of Jerusalem to the Babylonians

The captivity of Judah begins

The Babylonian Empire attained to its full extent under Nebuchadnezzar (604–561BC). It was funded by Nimrod (Genesis 10:10–11) and was the parent state of Assyria.

Assyria obtained the ascendency over Babylonia in the thirteenth century BC. From monuments discovered, it appears that the first capital of Assyria was not Nineveh but a city called by the name of the state, Asshur, situated 60 miles south of Nineveh. A more modern name of the spot is Kileh Sherghat. It was here that Pul (II Kings 15:19) and Tiglath Pileser (II Kings 15:29 and 16:7, etc.) must have had their seat of government in the first half of the eighth century. Sardanapalus I removed the seat of government to Nimrud, probably the Rosen of Genesis 10:12, about twenty miles below Nineveh. This must have been the capital when his son Shalmaneser brought away the captive Israelites in 721BC (II Kings 17:3 and 18:9). Sennacherib was the first Assyrian monarch who established Nineveh as a royal residence (702BC). It would thus appear that it was not the capital of Assyria in the time of Jonah (who must have been nearly a contemporary of Jeroboam II (825–773BC); see II Kings 14:25), great as it was then in extent and importance. The 'King of Nineveh 'mentioned in Jonah 3:6 may have been a viceroy. It was under Tiglath Pileser, Sargon (Isaiah 20:1) Sennacherib and Esarhaddon (II Kings 19:37 and Ezra 4:2), towards the end of the eighth century BC, that the Assyrian Empire reached its highest glory. At this time it extended to the River Halys and the Mediterranean in the west and to the Caspian Sea in the north. Esarhaddon appears to have made Babylon his residence for the last thirteen years of his reign, 680–667BC: it was during this period that Manasseh was brought before him and imprisoned (II Chronicles 33:11).

About 625BC, in the reign of Sardanapalus, the Babylonians along with the Medes having risen in rebellion, their combined

Nebuchadnezzar's statue

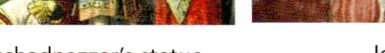

Jonah in Nineveh

forces sacked Nineveh and broke down the Assyrian power (Nahum 1, 2 and 3 and Ezekiel 31:3). Assyria proper now became a part of the Babylonian Empire.

It was under Nabopolassar and his son Nebuchadnezzar that the Chaldaeo-Babylonian Empire reached its highest point. The overthrow of Pharaoh Necho by Nebuchadnezzar (604BC) is noticed in Jeremiah 46:2 and II Kings 23:29. After this Nebuchadnezzar subdued Phoenicia and his forces took Jerusalem in 587. The glory of Babylon was now complete and realized the vision of the king as the golden head of the image whose 'breast and arms were of silver, his belly and thighs of brass, his legs of iron, and his feet part of iron and part of clay' (Daniel 2:32,28). Babylon was sacked by the Persians and the empire destroyed in 538BC.

Exile by the waters of Babylon

Daniel interprets the inscription in Babylon

The return from captivity

The dominions of Herod the Great were of nearly the same extent as those of Asamonaean kings: they included the Holy Land with the western part of what was then called Idumaea. The other part of Mumma formed a portion of the kingdom of Nabathaean Arabea. On the death of Herod, his dominions were divided between three of his sons:

Archelaus (Matthew 2:22), with the title of Ethnarch, ruled over Judea, Amaria and the western part of Idumaea.

Philip was Tetrarch of Ituraea and the region of Trachonitis that included Trachonitis proper, Batana, Auranitis, and Gaulanitis (Luke 3:1).

Antipas was styled Tetrarch of Galilee (Luke 3:1), but his dominions included Galilee and Peraea, i.e., the region beyond the River Jordan. (See Matthew 4:25, Mark 3:8 and John 10:40, etc.)

Archelaus was banished by the Roman government in AD12, and his territory was then made an imperial province, of which Pontius Pilate became procurator from AD26 to 36. Philip, whose name never appears in connection with the history of Christ, died in AD34. Antipas, is always called Herod in the Gospel of Luke (13:31 and 23:7, etc.), sometimes Herod the Tetrarch (Matthew 14:1 and Luke 3:9), and sometimes Herod the King (Matthew 14:9 and Mark 6:22,25). He was deposed by the Roman Emperor Caligula in AD40.

The dominions of all these rulers were again gathered up into a kingdom under Herod Agrippa I, the grandson of Herod the Great, in AD42. The political divisions marked on the map are those that existed during the public ministry of Jesus.

Arimathaea is named in no other connection than as the city of Joseph the 'honourable counsellor' (Matthew 26:57, Mark 15:43, Luke 23:51 and John 19:38). Two sites have been suggested as probable, one to the north, the other to the south of

Above: Herod the Great

Above right: Herod Agrippa, his grandson, interviews Paul

Right: the marriage at Cana when Jesus turned water into wine

The tomb arranged by Joseph of Arimathaea

The Three Wise Men arrive in Bethlehem

Jesus' triumphal entry into Jerusalem

Jesus sends out seventy disciples to spread the Word

Jesus before Pontius Pilate

Lydda. But the expression of Luke (23:51) as 'a city of the Jews' would seem to fix its position on the borders of the Samaritan region.

Caesarea, distinguished according to Josephus as Caesarea Augusta, was originally only a tower known as 'Strato's Tower', with a quay or landing-place. Herod the Great lavished large sums in improving its harbour and in adorning it as a royal residence. It afterwards became the Roman capital of Judaea and the official station of the procurators.

Caesarea Philippi is mentioned only in Matthew 16:13 and Mark 8:27. The site is supposed to have been situated close to one of the chief sources of the River Jordan, where according to tradition there was a cave dedicated to Pan.

Cana has been by old tradition identified with Kefr-Kenna, about four and a half miles northeast of Nazareth.

Decapolis (the region of the ten cities) is mentioned three times in the New Testament: Matthew 4:25, Mark 5:20 and 7:31. It is noticed by Pliny, Josephus and Ptolemy. Pliny observes that it is differently described by various writers, but he enumerates ten cities as belonging to it: Damascus, Philadelphia, Rhaphana, Scythopolis, Gadara, Hippos, Dion, Pella, Gelasa (Gerasa), and Calatha (Canatha). In the New Testament the name seems to express the southern portion of the Tetrarchy of Philip. In Matthew 15:25 it is expressly distinguished from Peraea, from Judaea and from Galilee, while the northern part of Philip's Tetrarchy seems to have been designated as 'the towns of Caesarea Philippi' (Mark 8:27); and in Mark 5:20, Decapolis evidently includes the neighbourhood of Gergesa.

Emmaus is said by Luke (24:13) to be sixty stadia from Jerusalem.

During Passion week, Jesus leaves Jerusalem for his lodging at Bethany

Feeding the five thousand

Jesus, Martha, Mary and Lazarus at Bethany

The walk to Emmaus

THE SEA OF GALILEE
MAP 10

Gennesaret (the Land of) is mentioned in Matthew 14:34 and Mark 6:53. It is a fertile, crescent-shaped plain on the northwest shore of the Lake of Gennesaret, about three miles in length and one in width. From its sheltered situation, and especially from its depression of more than 500 feet below sea level, its climate is of an almost tropical character. Josephus describes it as if it was an earthly paradise in which every useful plant grew and flourished.

Bethsaida (west) distinguished as 'Bethsaida of Galilee' (John 12:21) was in the land of Gennesaret (Mark 6:45) and near Capernaum and Chorazin (Matthew 11:21 and Luke 10:53).

Bethsaida (east), commonly known as Bethsaida Julias, is on the east side of the Jordan valley. In Luke 9:10 'the desert place' where the five thousand were fed, is said to belong 'to the city called Bethsaida'. That this city must have been on the side of the

lake opposite to Gennesaret is shown in the account of the same event given by Mark, in which we are told that 'the disciples, after the occurrence, crossed over to the other side unto Bethsaida' and 'came into the land of Gennesaret' (Mark 6:45,53). It is consistent, therefore, that they went from one Bethsaida to the other.

Capernaum, as the ordinary home of Christ during his public ministry, is the place of deepest interest of all the cities on the Lake of Gennesaret. But the question regarding its site is a very difficult one.

Gergesa, or Gergasa, is said by Origen to have been situated on the east shore of the lake.

Tiberias is mentioned in the New Testament only as giving to the lake one of its names and as the home of a portion of the five thousand who were fed by Christ on the other side of the lake (John 6:1,23 and 11:1).

Fishers of men

The great catch of fish

Walking on the waters

Calming the storm

Jesus teaching by the waterside

The risen Lord meets the disciples

ANCIENT JERUSALEM
MAPS 11 AND 12

Jerusalem stands upon an undulating piece of tableland which is surrounded on three sides by deep ravines and was originally divided into two unequal portions by a considerable depression that extended from south to north through the old city, and then turned to the west.

David's capture of Jerusalem

Of the three walls, the one that formed a complete circuit was as old as the time of David and Solomon, and it was strengthened by their successors. It enclosed only the two heights in which the old city stood, the other walls having been successively built to enclose the newer parts of the city that had been added on the north side.

The second wall reached over only a portion of the north side of the city. Starting towards the north from the gate called Gennath, after making two projecting angles it terminated at the tower Antonia.

The third wall was designed and partly built by Herod Agrippa. From the Tower of the Furnaces its general direction was along the Joppa road for nearly 1,000 feet; thence past the Royal Caverns to the 'Tomb of the Fuller', when it turned south and joined the old wall near the Pool of Bethesda. This wall encompassed the new city on three sides.

The name Jerusalem first occurs in the Bible as the capital of one of the Kings of the Amorites – Adoni-zedek – whom Joshua overcame and slew (Joshua 10:1–27). The tradition as generally received identifies the site of the Temple with the spot in 'the Land of Moriah' (Genesis 22:2) where Abraham offered up Isaac, and in accordance with II Chronicles 3:1. But doubts on the subject have existed from early times, and many now suppose that the offering up of Isaac took place on Mount Gerizim, and that the city of Melchizedek was the same as the Salim of John 3:23. If Jerusalem is the same as the capital of Melchizedek, there can be no doubt as to the origin of the latter part of the name. As the word in the Hebrew takes the dual form, it would seem to mean 'the two Salems', which would well agree with the topography of the ancient city, standing as it did upon two heights. It is stated in Joshua 15:63 that the Jebusites inhabited Jerusalem; they seem to have been regarded in the time of Adoni-zedek as a subordinate tribe belonging to the Amorites and were at times included under their name (Joshua 10:12).

Jerusalem was taken, smitten with the edge of the sword and set on fire by the Israelites after the conquest of Adonibezek (Judges 1:8). But Jebusites continued to dwell with the Israelites in the city (Joshua 15:63 and Judges 1:21) and held possession of

David at the threshing-floor, Jerusalem

The dedication of Solomon's temple

Miracle at the Pool of Siloam

Jerusalem at the time of the Crucifixion, a detail from "Panorama of Jerusalem and the Crucifixion of Jesus Christ" in *From Adam to Jesus* (TMP, 2016)

'the stronghold of Zion' when it was taken by David: 'Nevertheless, David took the stronghold of Zion; the same is the city of David.' 'So David dwelt in the fort and called it the city of David. And David built round about from Millo and increased (II Samuel 5:7, 9 and I Chronicles 11:4,5,8). Jerusalem now became the capital of the kingdom. However, the site of the Temple was still in the hands of the Jebusite chief Araunah, who had made peace with David and was on the most friendly terms with him, and from him it was obtained by purchase (II Samuel 24:16–25 and I Chronicles 21:15–28). The site of the Temple must at that time have been of less elevation than the northern part of Mount Moriah, probably standing in the relation to it of a small spur or terrace, with a still lower terrace (Ophel) extending beyond it to the south.

The walls of ancient Jerusalem

The Palaces

David dwelt for a while in the stronghold of the City of David, but he afterwards built for himself 'a house of cedar', and 'prepared a place for the Ark of God, and pitched for it a tent' in the City of David.

When the Temple was completed in the reign of Solomon, the priests brought up the Ark to place it in the Holy of Holies (I Kings 8:2,4 and II Chronicles 5:2). These expressions render it highly probable that David's house of cedar and the tent that he pitched for the Ark were situated on the lowest terrace of the hill Moriah, below the threshing-floor, but above the house of Obed-edom. The position of Ophel, the sloping ridge that was afterwards strengthened by Jotham and Manasseh (II Chronicles 27:3 and 33:14), answers to these conditions. But there is nothing to determine the exact site of the palace.

Solomon built a palace for himself called 'the palace of the fort of Lebanon' (II Chronicles 9:3,16). The house of Pharaoh's daughter seems to have adjoined this palace (I Kings 9:24 and II Chronicles 8:11). There is good reason to believe that it was situated upon Ophel, adjacent to the south side of the temple platform, at a lower level. It would thus seem that David's palace must have been to the south of Solomon's. The ascending subterranean passage under the temple platform, which still exists, possibly led from the palace to the Temple, and may have been 'the ascent by which the King went up to the house of the Lord', which was one of the things that particularly attracted the attention of the Queen of Sheba (I Kings 10:4,5).

The eastern gorge is uniformly called either the ravine of the Kedron or the torrent Kedron. In the Bible, 'brook' is used for 'torrent', both in the scripture and in Josephus (II Samuel 15:23, I Kings 2:37, II Kings 23:4,6 and John 18). A Jewish tradition, which can be traced to the fourth century, would identify the Kedron with 'the valley of Jehoshaphat' where, in the vision of the prophet, the nations were summoned to judgment (Joel 3:2,12).

The ravine that skirts the city on its west and south sides was known as the Valley of Hinnom or the Valley of the son of Hinnom in very early times (Joshua 15:8 and 18:16). Nothing is known of the origin of the name. A certain spot in it became notorious as a place of idolatrous worship in the days of Solomon and was called Tophet (II Kings 23:10, II Chronicles 28:3 and 33:6 and Isaiah 30:33). The portion of the valley where Tophet was situated seems to have been called the Lower Gihon.

En-rogel was a spring over which the boundary line passed (Joshua 15:7 and 18:6). Its situation may have been where the two ravines unite; but some would place it higher up the Kedron.

The fall of Jerusalem to Nebuchadnezzar

Nehemiah rebuilds Jerusalem's walls

The walls complete

The situation of Gihon is a question of some difficulty. It is first mentioned as the place where Solomon was annointed king, when the apprehensions of David, in his extreme old age, were excited on account of the conspiracy of Adonijah. The King was in his palace when he was informed of the sedition, and the conspirators were assembled at En-rogel. He commanded that Solomon should ride upon his own mule and be brought down to Gihon, that he should there be annointed, and that a shout should be raised, 'God save King Solomon!' accompanied by the blowing of trumpets. Joab, who was with Adonijah at En-rogel, heard the blast of the trumpets (I Kings 1:9,33,34,41). From this narrative it would seem that Gihon was at a lower level than the palace of David upon Ophel, that it was within a moderate distance of En-rogel, and that it was most likely not far from the palace. 'The well of Gihon', as it is called by Josephus in his narrative of these events, may as some have suggested be identified with the Pool of Siloam.

As far as the place of the proclamation of Solomon is concerned, the question presents no great difficulty. But there are two other passages that are less clear. In II Chronicles 32:30, it is said that Hezekiah 'stopped the upper water course of Gihon [more properly the waters of the Upper Gihon] and brought it straight down to the west side of the city of David'. From this it appears that there were two Gihons, an upper and a lower one. It has been supposed that this distinction refers to two pools, called on the map the Upper Pool (Serpents' Pool,) and the Lower Pool. Both these pools are on the west side of the city. But it seems more consistent to apply the term Upper Gihon, containing the 'Upper Pool', to the northern part of the valley of Hinnom, in distinction from the Lower Gihon, (I Kings 1:33,38) at the northeast corner of the city.

The Pool of Siloam is a reservoir supplied by a subterranean conduit from the Fountain of the Virgin. It is most likely 'the old pool' of Isaiah 22:11 and may have been constructed by David or Solomon. Just below it is the King's Pool, (Nehemiah 2:14) and 'the ditch' of Isaiah 22:11, which appears to have been a second pool made by Hezekiah 'between the two walls' to preserve the surplus water of Siloam for the use of the people, in the near prospect of the siege by the Assyrians.It is also supposed to be the 'Solomon's Pool' of Josephus.

PAUL'S JOURNEYS
MAP 13

Paul's escape from Damascus

The First Journey

Paul's first journey, in which he was accompanied by Barnabas, is described in Acts 13:4 and 14:28. They started from Antioch, embarked at Seleucia and sailed to Salamis, one of the chief cities of Cyprus. Having gone through the island, they came to Paphos, the residence of the deputy, Sergius Paulus. From Paphos they went to Perga in Pamphylia, where John Mark, who had accompanied them thus far, left them and returned to Jerusalem. The others then proceeded to Antioch in Pisidia. Driven out from there, they came to Icomum; and being again obliged to flee, they proceeded to Lystra and Derbe in Lycaonia, with 'the region that lieth round about'. They then turned back, doubling their way to Perga, and embarked at Attalia to return to Antioch. This journey appears to have occupied little more than a year, probably parts of AD47 and 48.

The Second Journey

The narrative of the second journey is given in Acts 15:36 and 18:22. After attending the council at Jerusalem, Paul and Barnabas returned to Antioch. However, when they were about to begin another journey they determined to separate owing to their difference respecting Mark. Paul took Silas as his companion, and 'went through Syria and Cilicia, confirming the churches'. He then proceeded, probably through the pass in Mount Taurus called the Cilician Gates, to Derbe and Lystra, when he invited Timothy to become his companion, and went through 'Phrygia and the region of Galatia'. Being forbidden by the Holy Ghost to preach the Word in Asia and Bithynia, he passed through Mysia to Troas, where he was joined by Luke. He was here summoned by a vision to pass over to Macedonia and sailed by Samothracia to Neapolis. From there he went on to Philippi, where he abode 'certain days'. Luke appears to have left the party there. Paul, with Silas and Timothy, pursued his journey through Amphipolis and Apollonia to Thessalonica, the capital of the province of Macedonia, where he remained for three weeks.

After spending some short time at Berea, Paul went by sea to Athens, leaving Silas and Timothy to follow him. He spent a short time there before going on to Corinth, where he spent a year and a half and appears to have written the First and Second Epistles to the Thessalonians. Intending to keep the approaching feast of Pentecost at Jerusalem, he embarked from Cenchrea, one of the two seaports of Corinth, for Ephesus. Priscilla and Aquila accompanied him thus far. Making a very short stay at Ephesus, he sailed for Caesarea, and when he had 'gone up' (that is, up to Jerusalem) and saluted the Church, he returned to Antioch. This second journey appears to have occupied something less than three years, from the autumn of AD51 to the spring of AD54.

Paul preaching

Paul embarks

Paul's vision in Macedonia

Paul preaches in Athens

Barnabas, who accompanied Paul on his early journeys

Paul meets Sergius Paulus, proconsul of Cyprus

The Third Journey

The third journey is given in Acts 18:23 and 21:17. From Antioch the apostle went over 'all the country of Galatia and Phrygia in order'. It is probable that he followed the great line of traffic from Antioch through Tarsus, his native place, the capital of Cilicia, and Caesarea Mazaca, called also Caesarea ad Argaeum, the capital of Cappadocia, to Tavia, the easternmost of the chief Galatian cities. He passed on to Ephesus, where he remained for three years, and probably wrote the Epistle to the Galatians and the First Epistle to the Corinthians. Taking his leave of Ephesus, he sailed to Troas, and remained there a short time in the hope that Titus would join him. He then proceeded to Macedonia, where Titus came to him, and most probably made some stay at Philippi. Luke says that, having 'gone over those parts', he went to Greece. It is highly probable that at this time he prolonged his journey and 'preached the Gospel of Christ round about unto Illyricum'.

In Greece he abode three months and wrote the Epistle to the Romans, spending as we may suppose most of the time at Corinth. He proposed to return to Syria directly, as he had done during his second journey but was induced to go by way of Macedonia. He was accompanied by Timothy and six other disciples and probably took the regular road through Berea, Thessalonica, and Amphipolis to Philippi. Here he was joined by Luke and sent on the companions who had thus far travelled with him to Troas. Having rejoined the party, he remained at Troas for seven days. His companions embarked from there, but he himself walked on for about nine miles, to Assos, where they took him on board. They then went by Mitylene, Chios, Samos, and Trogyllium to Miletus, where Paul sent for the elders of the Ephesian Church and took his solemn farewell of them. They called at Coos and Rhodes on the voyage to Patara, one of the seaports of Lycia, where they left the ship that appears to have conveyed them from Troas and embarked in another for Tyre. Here again they took ship for Ptolemais, and Caesarea, where they stayed some days with Philip the evangelist, and then completed their journey to Jerusalem by land. This third

Priscilla, wife of Aquila, tent-makers of Corinth

Paul provokes riots in Ephesus, led by the silversmith Demetrius

Paul imprisoned in Caesarea

journey appears to have occupied nearly four years, from the summer of AD54 to the spring of AD58.

Paul's Voyage from Caesarea to Rome
(Acts16)

Paul was sent by Claudius Lysias from Jerusalem to Caesarea by Antipatris. When it was determined that he should go to Rome, he embarked with other prisoners under the charge of Julius the Centurion in a trading ship of Adramyttium, a seaport of Mysia. They touched at Sidon, sailed to the north of Cyprus owing to contrary winds from the west and, passing the coasts of Cilicia and Pamphylia, came to Myra, the chief seaport of Lycia. It is likely that the ship of Adramyttium now turned homewards towards the north.

Julius and the prisoners re-embarked in a ship from Alexandria – probably one of many that were then employed in conveying corn from Alexandria to Italy, a large number of which discharged their cargoes at Puteoli. It would seem that this ship, in accordance with a custom that experience had recommended in ancient navigation, when her direct course was opposed by strong westerly winds, had made her passage from Alexandria to Myra, where she could take advantage of a favourable current. The weather did not improve, and they were 'many days' in sailing 130 miles, when they found themselves off Cnidus. They here lost the favourable current that sets to the west from Myra to Cnidus and, being still kept back by the west wind, they made for Crete, rounding Cape Salmone with a view, as it would seem, to get on as well as they could under the lee of the island. They advanced to a seaport called Fair Havens, near the city of Lasea. Paul advised that they should remain there till the stormy season was past, but it was determined by the centurion, in accordance with the

opinion of the pilot and the owner of the ship, that they should try to get on to Phoenice (or Phoenix, as it should be called), the harbour of which was supposed to be a better place of shelter than Fair Havens, being secured by the land from all the westerlies, whether they inclined to the north or the south.

When they started from Phoenix, 'the south wind blew softly', but there presently arose a hurricane from the east-northeast, formerly called in those seas

Paul sails to Cyprus en route to Rome

Euroclydon and in modern times a Levanter. They were compelled to scud before the gale and were driven towards the little island of Clauda. Under the lee of the land, they managed to take in the boat that they had towed from Fair Havens, reckoning on the continuance of the gentle south wind with which they had started. They were now in dread in case, overpowered by the wind, they should be driven as far as the quicksands of the Syrtis.

Assuming that the wind continued to blow from the east-northeast, a vessel would be drifted to the west-northwest, which in this case would be from Clauda to Malta. And indeed, at length the ship was driven on the island of Melita (now known as Malta).

After remaining there for three months, Paul and his companions embarked in another ship of Alexandria, called the *Castor and Pollux*. They touched at Syracuse and 'fetching a compass' in consequence of adverse winds, reached Rhegium, where they waited a day for a fair wind to carry them through the Strait of Messina to Puteoli. From here Paul proceeded to Rome along the Appian Way, where he was met by some of the brethren who came to meet him as far as the Tree Taverns and the Forum of Appius. It appears that he sailed from Caesarea in the autumn and reached Rome in the early spring.

Shipwrecked on Melita (Malta)

To Rome along the Appian Way

Paul's final imprisonment, in Rome